Y0-BRR-946

Lost City in the Clouds

Lost City in the Clouds

THE DISCOVERY OF
MACHU PICCHU

by ELIZABETH GEMMING · illustrated by MIKE EAGLE

Coward, McCann and Geoghegan, Inc.
New York

Text copyright © 1980 by Elizabeth Gemming
Illustrations copyright © 1980 by Mike Eagle
All rights reserved. This book, or parts thereof, may not be reproduced
in any form without permission in writing from the publishers.
Published simultaneously in Canada by Academic Press Canada Limited, Toronto (formerly
Longman Canada Limited).
"The Explorer" from *Rudyard Kipling's Verse: Definitive Edition*.
Reprinted by permission of Doubleday & Company, Inc.
Library of Congress Cataloging in Publication Data
Gemming, Elizabeth.   Lost city in the clouds.
Bibliography: p.
SUMMARY: An account of Hiram Bingham's 1911
discovery of a well-preserved Incan city perched
between two peaks of the Andes mountains.
1. Machu Picchu, Peru—Juvenile literature.
[1. Machu Picchu, Peru.   2. Incas.   3. Bingham, Hiram.
1875-1956.   4. Indians of South America]   I. Eagle,
Michael   II. Title.
F3429.1.M3G45   985'.3   78-31877
ISBN 0-698-30698-8
PRINTED IN THE UNITED STATES OF AMERICA

For Michael and Alexia Prichard,
whose mother is from the land of the Incas

CONTENTS

AUTHOR'S NOTE

The term *Inca* originally referred to the emperor only. The Spanish colonists used the word to refer to the emperor and the royal family. Today, we use *Inca* to refer to a remarkable civilization of early Peru and call its people the Incas.

Vilcapampa is the old spelling of the legendary lost city of the Incas. Vilcabamba is the modern Spanish spelling of the Peruvian river of that name.

Conversations in this book are imaginary. Working from Hiram Bingham's own descriptions of his discoveries, I have tried to convey his enthusiasm, curiosity, and lively personality through passages of fictional dialogue.

FOREWORD

The astonishing story of Hiram Bingham's discovery of Machu Picchu begins 11,200 feet above sea level, in Cuzco, Peru. Nestled in a lofty green valley in the Andes Mountains, Cuzco is the oldest inhabited city in the Americas. It has survived looting by the Spanish *conquistadores* who invaded it in 1533, and it has recovered from two devastating earthquakes. As the ancient capital of the fabled Inca empire, Cuzco is one of the marvels of the world.

When Hiram Bingham first explored the narrow streets and wide plazas of Cuzco, in 1909, he was not a famous archaeologist, but only a young history professor from Yale University with no specialized knowledge of the early civilizations of South America. Eventually, he became one of the foremost authorities on the vast Inca empire, for he discovered—almost by accident—its spectacular citadel, a remote mountain retreat hidden for hundreds of years by dense jungle growth.

Bingham's stay in Cuzco was part of a dream come true—his cherished plan to retrace the old Spanish colonial trade routes through the Central Andes.

On his first visit to South America, in 1906, Bingham followed in the footsteps of Simón Bolívar, a revolutionary hero who had crossed the Andes from Venezuela to Colombia during military campaigns that lasted from 1816 to 1824. Bolívar, known as the Great Liberator, or the George Washington of South America, had freed much of the northern part of the continent from Spanish rule.

Barely home from his Andean expedition, Bingham was already longing to return. He had fallen under the magic spell of the majestic peaks and passes, the glaciers and the lush valleys so far below, in the highest mountain range on earth after the towering Himalayas of Asia. Bingham had sensed the enchantment of high mountains since childhood. Born in the Hawaiian Islands in 1875, he had gone on his first mountain-climbing expedition on the island of Maui at the age of four, with his missionary father.

And now, his dream was coming true! His inborn love of adventure and his scholarly turn of mind had conspired to bring him back to the Andes. Young Professor Bingham's written account of his 1906 journey had so favorably impressed Elihu Root, then the United States Secretary of State, that Root had appointed Bingham an official delegate to the first Pan American Scientific Congress, to be held in Santiago, Chile, in December 1908.

Hiram Bingham realized that his official standing as a United States delegate would help him attain his goal of investigating the Andean trade routes. And that was why he was in Cuzco one damp day to meet with prominent local officials.

Lost City in the Clouds

1. In the Land of the Incas

January 1909. Hiram Bingham closed the city guidebook he had been reading and leaned against the wall of a massive stone building to catch his breath. At Cuzco's two-mile-high altitude, the atmosphere was so thin it made him dizzy. While he rested, Bingham ran his fingers over the wall of the house. The rock wall was strange to the touch, crafted of huge, many-sided stones that had been polished smooth and fitted together without mortar. Not even the thinnest blade of his penknife could be wedged between the stones, so precisely were they matched and fitted!

This Spanish-style house, like most of the churches, palaces, monasteries, and convents of Cuzco. was constructed on the remains of ancient Inca foundation walls.

Hiram Bingham watched an Andean woman hurry past. She was bundled in a long, full, red skirt and a black-and-red woollen shawl held together with a simple metal pin. She called to another woman in a language he had never heard before—he wondered if it was Quechua, the Inca language still spoken by many thousands of people in the

15

Andes. The two women walked on and talked excitedly on their way to market, their fingers busily working portable spindles.

With a little time left for sightseeing, Bingham ducked down a narrow alley, dodging caravans of pack llamas driven by stocky beardless men dressed in short trousers and brightly colored ponchos. Like the women, they were also on their way to the open market in Cuzco's main plaza. Stopping to catch his breath once more, Bingham envied these sturdy mountain people, whose unusually large lungs could easily take in great reserves of the oxygen-poor air. These mountain folk of Cuzco were descendants of the Incas, the living heritage of that brilliant civilization whose vast Andean empire had stretched more than 2,500 miles, from Ecuador, in the northern part of South America, all the way to Chile.

The Inca empire had been efficiently organized and fabulously wealthy, a powerful empire of sun worshipers that had come to a sudden and tragic end nearly 400 years before. As a history teacher, Bingham found himself intrigued by the mystery of the Incas' destiny. How and why had one small tribe from the valley around Cuzco abruptly begun to expand their power, spreading their religion, laws, customs, and language until they had created an empire that rivaled that of the Romans?

Bingham had read that an Inca king, Pachacuti, began during the 1400s to conquer territory and win influence far beyond Cuzco. Pachacuti, whose name meant "He Who Transforms the Earth," adopted the crown-like fringe, or *borla,* of a sacred sovereign. He laid down simple laws for his people: do not lie, do not steal, do not be lazy.

From what Bingham could see of the gentle, industrious folk streaming through the lanes of Cuzco, those laws were still very much observed.

The Incas had been gifted city planners, engineers and stonemasons, wise lawgivers, and skilled farmers and plant and livestock breeders. They were a proud, honest, and obedient people who probably did not understand—until too late—the fierce greed of a small band of Spanish adventurers who landed on the Peruvian coast in 1532. The Spanish leader, Francisco Pizarro, commanding some 160 foot soldiers and horsemen, managed through treachery, cunning, and appalling cruelty to bring down the mighty Inca empire. Within a couple of years, Pizarro seized all its golden treasures and enslaved millions of bewildered subjects.

Bingham bent his head and walked faster as a gust of cold wind howled around the corner of the Church of Santo Domingo. He kept reminding himself that although it was summer in the Andes (where the seasons, below the Equator, are the reverse of ours), temperatures in this mountain climate always ranged from bracing to bitter cold. It was not surprising that the Incas had worshiped the Sun.

It seemed only right to Bingham that the Church of Santo Domingo and its convent rested on the gracefully curved walls of the sacred Inca Temple of the Sun, here in this ancient city of emperors. In this temple, as in other temples in the vast empire, the feast of Inti-raymi, or Midwinter's Day, had been celebrated annually on the shortest day of the year. Just as the days were about to grow longer, the emperor, borne on a golden litter, led a procession of nobles and officials into the Golden Enclosure of the Temple of the Sun, where there was a magnificent "garden" of plants and animals—cornstalks and llamas—sculpted of purest gold. White llamas were sacrificed to the sun, and at the moment of daybreak, priests threw kisses to the god and attempted to tether him to a stone pillar, the *Intihuatana*—Hitching Post of the Sun.

Shivering in the wind, Bingham could picture the people on Midwinter's Day, frozen with fear that Inti, their lord and protector, would withdraw ever farther, finally vanishing behind a bank of black clouds at nightfall—never to return.

O Sun! Do not leave us, for we are thy children!
O Sun! Do not abandon us to perish in the cold and the dark!

Inca soothsayers had long observed the shadows on the great stone sundials in their mountain temples, and they did not share the people's anguish. They alone, following a solar calendar of four seasons, knew how to calculate exactly when the sun was about to turn and begin its long journey back to the land of the Incas.

But the common people greeted the sun's annual return as a miracle. Rejoicing, they believed the Sun God had heard their heartfelt prayers. They celebrated Inti-raymi with feasting, singing, and dancing to the music of flutes, horns, bells, and drums.

Because the Inca emperor was considered the son of the Sun, everything on earth belonged to him. It was his sacred duty to take care of his people and to keep them content throughout their lives by providing food, clothing, shelter, and justice for all. They, in turn, dutifully planted and harvested crops, herded llamas and alpacas, wove cloth, worked in gold and silver mines and stone quarries, and helped construct countless roads, public buildings, and aqueducts.

Yet, Bingham reminded himself, they were not slaves. No, the people, millions of them, worked in a spirit of joy and pride as they performed the yearly stint of labor each one of them owed to their generous master, the son of the Sun.

What a remarkable civilization! As a student and teacher of history, Bingham was intrigued by these unique people, for in all their conquests they had not destroyed the traditions of those they conquered, but rather had learned from them. The disciplined Inca culture had rested on a much older heritage, in fact, on several ancient foundations. The Incas had learned from the master architects of a

1,000-year-old Indian culture of the *altiplano*, a dizzyingly high plateau near Lake Titicaca, as well as from the master goldsmiths, potters, and weavers of the mysterious desert kingdoms on the seacoast of Peru.

Bingham was lost in thought. Suddenly, from all over Cuzco, church bells began to ring, resounding in the thin mountain air. Startled, he glanced at his watch. He would have to hurry or he would be late for his appointment with the city dignitaries.

As he strode along, he remembered how often Secretary of State Root had impressed upon the delegates to the Scientific Congress the importance of goodwill and friendship. It would never do to insult the officials by being late, for South Americans were unfailingly gracious and hospitable.

2. A Goodwill Mission

Just on time, the young professor from the United States was welcomed warmly. Among the dignitaries gathered to meet him was the prefect of the mountain province of Apurímac. This man, J. J. Nuñez, had braved the worst rainy season in twenty-five years in order to tell Bingham about certain Inca ruins in his district.

"These ruins, Professor Bingham, are at a place called Choq-quequirau, which means Cradle of Gold. I am certain that this ruined city is the legendary place known as Vilcapampa the Old, the last stronghold of the Incas."

"You mean the secret Inca capital following the Spanish Conquest?"

"Precisely! You see, the Inca emperor Manco II fled Cuzco ahead of Pizarro and escaped over the mountains with his family and many followers. They took with them many loads of woollen clothing, the mummies of his royal ancestors, and the golden image of the Sun from the temple at Cuzco. In a secret hideaway, it is said, they managed to hide their gold and silver and jewels from the Spanish *conquistadores*." Nuñez paused. "That treasure has *never been found!*"

Nuñez was wild to find the lost treasure of the Incas—in fact, all Peru seemed to have caught treasure fever.

Bingham was fascinated, though as a scholar he was not so much attracted by rumors of buried treasure as by the secrets of the past. He had indeed heard tales of a "lost city in the clouds" which the Spanish soldiers had frantically searched for but never discovered.

"Please, Professor Bingham, promise me you will come to my province to see the Cradle of Gold!"

Nuñez eagerly described the city: it lay higher even than Cuzco, at an altitude of 12,000 feet behind a range of towering peaks, on the rainy eastern slopes of the Andes above the bamboo jungles and headwaters of the mighty Amazon River. Instantly, Bingham's mind was filled with memories of Maui, the Hawaiian paradise he loved so much—his childhood home. He longed for peaks and flowers and tropical streams, and he thought, too, of one of his favorite poems, Rudyard Kipling's "The Explorer":

> Something hidden. Go and find it. Go and look behind
> the ranges—
> Something lost behind the Ranges. Lost and waiting for
> you. Go!

Nuñez was talking faster and faster. ". . . and only a few persons have ever managed to cross the Apurímac rapids and reach the ruins. I recently led a party of treasure hunters to the place myself. It took us weeks just to hack out a path—twelve miles through the jungle! We knew that a Frenchman, years ago, had turned up a few bones and some pottery. And what did we find? A small bronze crowbar, some clay pots and grinding stones for maize, and a few bronze shawl pins, nothing more. Still, I am absolutely certain there is treasure hidden at the Cradle of Gold! Your personal recommendation, Professor Bingham, would enable me to persuade the President of Peru to order excavations at once!"

"But Señor Nuñez, you flatter me. I am a historian, not an archaeologist. I don't see how. . . ."

Nuñez held up his hand. "Ah, you are too modest, Professor Bingham," he laughed. "You have a doctoral degree, you have been honored by your government. Do not refuse this mission, it will be the experience of a lifetime."

24

Bingham hesitated. He longed to explore the Andes, and he did have the time for such a trip. But he knew that the rainy season was the worst possible time for a journey to a remote section of these dangerous mountains. It would be not only wet but bitter cold, with temperatures seldom above freezing. And then, down in the jungle, it would be brutally hot and humid. Yet, these very hazards challenged his sense of adventure. He liked Nuñez, too, and suspected the man simply wouldn't take no for an answer. The prefect had exaggerated his scholarly qualifications, of course, but among the people of Apurímac, there would surely be some who could tell him many exciting details about the Incas and their way of life.

"All right, Señor Nuñez, I'll have a look at your Inca city."

Nuñez clapped his hands with delight. "Excellent, excellent," he cried. "I shall leave my aide here in Cuzco to give you any assistance you might need. I myself must return at once to Apurímac, but I shall expect to see you again there in a short time."

On February 1, 1909, Hiram Bingham left Cuzco in the pouring rain. With him were a friend, Clarence L. Hay; two Peruvian soldier-escorts provided by Nuñez; and a mule driver with a train of pack mules. Just outside of town, they passed a massive gray fortress, on the bluff overlooking Cuzco.

"So that's Sacsahuaman," exclaimed Bingham, peering through the mist. "I've never seen anything so magnificent!" He turned to one of the soldiers. "When was it built?"

"We are not certain—perhaps 500 years ago, to defend Cuzco

against marauding tribes from the jungles beyond the mountains where we are heading. It is said that 20,000 men labored eighty years to finish it. I find it beautiful—do you see how the stones grow smaller toward the top of the wall? The largest stones, at the very bottom, weigh 200, even 300 tons," the soldier explained.

"Incredible! The stones are huge, many-sided, oddly angled, and yet the effect is so graceful, the pattern so pleasing. I'm amazed that the Incas were able to cut stone so precisely. Isn't it true that they had only the simplest of tools—small crowbars and grass ropes—and measured by eye alone?"

"Yes, Señor, as far as we know," the soldier replied, "and the stone was quarried at least a mile or more from Cuzco, for none is found in the city itself. My ancestors had no knowledge of the wheel, so naturally they had no carts, and the llama is too weak to carry more than eighty to one hundred pounds." The soldier shrugged. "It is a mystery."

"Why, of course! I had forgotten," exclaimed Clarence Hay. "The horse was unknown in the Andes before Pizarro brought the first ones from Spain."

Bingham nodded. "The Incas were terrified of horses, and Pizarro was quick to take advantage of this. He ordered his cavalry soldiers to prance and buck their horses, and with fewer than two hundred men, Pizarro managed to frighten hundreds of thousands of Inca soldiers into submission. Not even a fortress like Sacsahuaman was able to save the empire."

Hay stared back at the fortress for a moment. "And this gigantic place was built entirely by the power of human muscle?"

26

"It seems so. I have been told that, among some 12 million people in the empire, there were possibly 6 million occupied in public works. Then, as now, an Andean farmer needs to spend only about sixty days a year in planting, tending, and harvesting his garden. A huge project such as Sacsahuaman kept many people too busy to become restless, and it served to remind them of the military might of their rulers. Today, though, the people of Cuzco use this monument mainly for festivals and picnics."

By now, Sacsahuaman was far behind, no longer visible through the rain. The wind blew relentlessly as the men and mules crossed a swampy, treeless plain on a stony Inca road. They skirted several great agricultural terraces, and Bingham could see how wheeled wagons would have been next to useless in such rough terrain, even if the Incas had known how to build them.

When evening came, they spent the night in an Indian village. They dined on *cuy,* a large guinea pig, roasted over a wood fire, and on boiled *chuñu,* white potatoes preserved by an age-old method of freeze-drying in cold mountain air. With their supper, they drank cup after cup of steaming hot tea.

Clarence Hay turned to one of the Peruvian soldier-guides. "Tell me, Sergeant, isn't it true that the Incas did not really know much about astronomy—compared, say, to the Mayas of Central America, or to the Arabs? I'm very interested in the Mayas, and I somehow expected the Incas to be more like them."

"I do not think they were," the soldier replied. "They worshiped spirits in the thunder, lightning, and water, and, I suppose, the moon and stars. But the sun gave them life itself."

The wind roared steadily around the little huts of the settlement.

28

Bingham looked thoughtful. "It's interesting, I find, that people who live in hot climates would naturally welcome the coolness of the night, and tend to observe and worship what they can see only by night: the moon and the stars against the blackness beyond. But here in the Andes, the night would seem to stand not for beauty and comfort but for cold and disease, even death."

"Yes," nodded the soldier, "the dark is our enemy, but the sun is our friend. That is why the *Intihuatana*, the Hitching Post of the Sun that stood in every temple, was so sacred. When Pizarro's men realized how important these sundials were to my people, they broke them off. I have never seen a single one that is still standing."

By now the campfire was burning low, and the shadows of an Andean night flickered in the corners of the hut. All at once, the men swallowed the last of their tea and prepared to sleep.

The next morning, they continued their trek. They hiked down through green and fragrant valleys dotted with yellow flowers and tall agave plants, past fields of pale-green sugar cane. After fording several rain-swollen streams and descending a tricky winding trail on muleback, they reached the Apurímac River canyon and crossed it by a modern bridge.

On the other side, they entered a marvelous landscape of deep-green wooded slopes and icy waterfalls, all the more gorgeous under a bright sun that broke through the rain for an hour or two. Soon, though, their route left behind this lush valley of cacti, lantanas, irises, and parrots, to climb once again to the highlands. Shivering in a chilly drizzle at 13,000 feet, Bingham and Hay found themselves on the border between the temperate zone and the tropics. They were gazing down on a sea of blossoms and canefields, and up—perhaps to 20,000 feet—at a sea of forbidding, blue-white glaciers!

"Isn't it fantastic!" Bingham exclaimed. "It's like seeing the South Pole and the Equator all at one time."

A mile outside the town of Abancay, they saw Nuñez and his sugar-planter friends, who had clattered out on horseback to escort them to their lodgings. That night there was a banquet in their honor. In Abancay, as in every village and town in Peru, the North Americans were warmed by the kindness and generosity of everyone they met.

"Ah, Señor Bingham, Señor Hay, it is good to see you," said Nuñez. "You must know by now that there is much more to the land of the Incas than Cuzco! But then, wandering over the mountains is in the tradition of the Andes."

"What do you mean, Señor Nuñez?" asked Hay.

"I refer to the legend that tells of the origin of the Incas. I will tell you! The first Inca, Manco Capac, and his sister-wife, Mama Ocllo, were born, so the story goes, on the Island of the Sun in Lake Titicaca. The creator-god, Viracocha, told them to go forth with a sacred llama and a golden staff, and to found a city at a place where the staff would sink out of sight in the fertile earth. They did so, and they called their city Cuzco, which means 'navel' or 'heart' in the Quechua language.

"Manco then went north and his wife went south, to teach their people agriculture and the household arts, as well as industrious habits and virtuous ways. And so the kingdom of the Incas was founded—it is a beautiful story, I think." Nuñez puffed on his pipe. "But now, you must get some rest, for tomorrow will not be easy."

3. The Cradle of Gold

The next day, the rain came down in torrents. Yet always, there were those magical glimpses of canefields and flowers veiled in the mist—blue and pink patches amid the softly glowing green.

The muddy trail descended to the place where they had to cross the Apurímac for the second time. They were very close to Choqquequirau, the Cradle of Gold, in a landscape so wild and rugged that Bingham could easily understand why it was a likely place for a secret hideout. By five o'clock in the afternoon, they could already hear the booming of the 250-foot-wide river, the Great Speaker, thundering through its canyon 7,000 feet below!

The sun had long since set behind the walls of the gorge. The mules, trembling with fright, began to pick their way over fallen trees down a trail loosened by avalanches, heading toward camp. In the dark, Bingham and Hay blindly followed their guides around hairpin turns, each turn with either a chasm or a plunging cataract at the bend. It seemed an eternity until Bingham finally spotted the flickering lights of two modest reed huts in a mimosa thicket. When the camp master tried to welcome the exhausted men, the Great Speaker drowned out every word he said.

In the early morning, Bingham and Hay had their first look at the rapids. The river had risen fifty feet in the heavy rains and was tearing by at breakneck speed.

A frail-looking suspension bridge, swaying in the wind, looped down to within twenty-five feet of the churning waves—a swinging catwalk some 275 feet long and only three feet wide, bathed in icy spray.

Hay looked worried. "Is *that* the only way across?"

"It is, but it's safe enough," said Bingham. "The cables are now made of wire instead of the hand-twisted vines the Incas used. There has been a bridge at this spot for 500 or 600 years—the ancient Inca bridge finally collapsed about twenty years ago. There is a book I have back home with a wonderful picture of it—in fact, that picture is one of the reasons why I wanted so badly to come to Peru," said Bingham.

"How could a bridge made of *vines* last hundreds of years?"

"Well, every two years the bridges were repaired and the cables replaced—cables as thick as a man's body. Bridge repairing was an important duty, and the bridges were so prized that anyone caught damaging or destroying one was put to death. It's no exaggeration to say that without the bridge at this very spot, there would have been no empire, for once the Incas were across the Apurímac, they expanded northward tremendously fast."

Hay turned to look at the bridge. "Then Pizarro's men must have used the bridges too."

"Yes. Because the Incas were reluctant to destroy their bridges, the

33

Spaniards were able to penetrate the Central Andes with relative ease—although altitude sickness nearly finished them off."

"How many miles of roads did the Incas build? Governing an empire as vast as theirs must have been very difficult," Hay concluded.

"Communications were all-important in keeping the empire under tight control. Can't you just see armies on the march, swift relay runners carrying parcels and messages, llama caravans with bundles of woollen cloth and sacks of maize and potatoes! There were thousands of miles of roads—this bridge was a vital link on the Royal Road, which wound 3,250 miles through the Andes. The Incas called a bridge 'little brother of the road.' "

"I thought the Incas had no writing system, Bingham. How did they send messages?" Hay asked.

"By a very elaborate system of knotted woollen cords, dyed in various colors, called *quipus*. These cords conveyed accounts, inventories of everything from llamas to weapons, and population censuses. Only specially trained readers could decipher them. The relay runners were constantly on the go, keeping far-flung parts of the empire in touch with Cuzco, the capital. To deaden cold, hunger, and fatigue, the runners were allowed to chew the leaves of the *coca* plant, a narcotic forbidden to ordinary people. The runners even carried fresh fruit from the jungle and fresh fish from the Pacific Ocean, more than one hundred miles from Cuzco, to grace the emperor's table! But look, here come our porters. Let's go!"

The Indian bearers crept across the bridge on all fours. Bingham and Hay followed, inch by inch, not daring to look down. Below them, instant death awaited in freezing currents that would dash them against the rocks. The pack mules had to be left in camp, for the rest of the journey was to be made on foot.

They were, by now, a mile above sea level, and the Cradle of Gold was situated another mile higher, and almost straight up. Bingham and Hay scaled ancient stone paths that were more like ladders, and crossed streams on slippery log bridges, ever higher.

Not used to the altitude, they became dizzy and short of breath as they crawled along, and they had to stop and rest every fifty feet. Yet as he lay panting by the trail, Bingham was enchanted. He thought that he had never before seen anything so magnificent. In the far distance, incredible snow-capped peaks pierced the clouds and emerged above them, rising another 6,000 feet. The river thundered below, at the foot of sheer precipices scarred by rockslides and dotted with clumps of foliage and flowers. All around, green jungle mingled with a maze of forested slopes. *Something lost behind the Ranges. Lost and waiting for you.* This, Bingham felt, was only the beginning!

The two young explorers had their first glimpse of Choqquequirau in the early afternoon, from a bold headland 6,000 feet above the river. They took a drink from a nearby waterfall and settled down on a patch of flat ground to marvel at the majestic terraced city that lay before them.

The Cradle of Gold was a typical Inca stronghold, stunningly located on the saddle of a mountain spur high above a river gorge. It enjoyed a panoramic view, and was surrounded by precipices—it would be easy to defend and very difficult to invade. Great contoured terraces, connected by stone stairways and drainage ditches, still retained precious soil. What skillful farmers the Incas were to construct garden terraces where there was so little land for farming—and to make plants grow at all at such altitudes!

"Good Lord, Bingham, watch out!" screamed Hay. They stared in horror at a giant condor descending in ever-narrowing circles directly above them, its beak and talons poised in readiness.

They buried their heads in their arms—but the condor wheeled and soared away, as suddenly as it had appeared.

"That bird must have had a wingspread of twelve feet! A condor can carry away a live sheep. Close call, Hay—come on, let's find a place to spend the night. Tomorrow is another day."

36

It had been extremely hot and humid, and the two inexperienced explorers had given all their gear to the Indian bearers. Now the bearers were far behind, and Bingham and Hay had not so much as a knapsack. At their present altitude, it was wet and bitter cold. They spent the night, almost sleepless, huddled together in a makeshift nest of dry grasses inside a tiny abandoned thatch-roofed hut.

But morning came, and so did the bearers. The party eagerly clambered the rest of the way up the ridge to explore the Cradle of Gold. Bingham had carefully studied his copy of the Royal Geographic Society's *Hints to Travellers*, a British handbook, and had learned that good archaeologists take photographs and measurements, draw sketches and rough maps, and take pains to describe everything they find as accurately as possible.

The two men found the ruins already nicely cleared by Nuñez and his treasure hunters. One cluster of buildings had had a parapet with a glorious view of the river—a silver ribbon far below—along with cliffs and waterfalls, forests and snow peaks. There were two windowless structures, long rectangular buildings of impressive size.

"Look here, Hay, no windows. The Incas were superstitious and feared the night air, thinking it carried disease."

"After last night, I can believe it too!"

Bingham laughed. "Say, look at that grassy hilltop at the end of the saddle, sort of leveled off. A sentry post, no doubt. And look up there—a dried-up watercourse. There's the main plaza, and there's a cistern for glacial meltwater. Water was important, both for irrigation and for drinking and cooking. In this high and dry altitude the human body really craves liquids, and I'm sure the Incas were no different from the Andeans of today—they ate a lot of soups and stews, and they made *chicha,* a beer from sprouted maize. I wonder if we'll find any pottery."

They walked around a group of crudely built houses made of fieldstone set in clay, surrounding the central plaza. These houses were in sharp contrast to the beautifully polished walls and doorways of the long palaces.

Beside a gigantic staircase, a huge rock faced east, where the sun rose. There, surely, the Inca priests had gathered at break of day to worship and throw kisses to their god!

There seemed to be numerous storehouses in the network of steps and narrow alleys, but all were empty. Below the lowest of the garden terraces, Bingham discovered some small, simple burial caves contain-

ing heaps of bones that did not appear ever to have been covered with earth. The Indian guides and bearers, who had been watching Bingham and Hay taking notes with much interest, became nervous when the two began measuring bones. They retreated, upset by the presence of the spirits of their ancestors.

Bingham could picture those long-dead men and women in their neat one-and-a-half-story houses. The houses had steep gables and stone pegs for anchoring thatched roofs on these windswept heights. Though the simple houses were empty, Bingham could picture the people sitting or sleeping on the earth floor on piles of blankets of llama or alpaca wool—their only furniture.

He noticed stone wall pegs alternating with cupboard-like niches, and imagined the people hanging ponchos or *chicha* jars on the pegs or storing pots and dishes in the niches. In one niche, Bingham found a part from a small hand spindle, hundreds of years old but exactly like those he had seen Andean women using as they walked to market in Cuzco.

Bingham and Hay spent four days on the mountain site of the Cradle of Gold, enveloped in rain or mist the whole time, and then returned to Cuzco the way they had come. On the way, they had to report to Nuñez that they had not found any treasure and did not think there was any to be found. Nuñez was greatly disappointed, but still convinced that "his" city would one day prove to be Vilcapampa the Old.

For Hiram Bingham, it was time to return to Yale. But he was captivated by the legend of the lost city of the Incas and was beginning to wonder whether that fabled city might lie *beyond* the distant peaks he had seen from the Cradle of Gold. He vowed to return to search for the ruins of the last Inca capital, the Lost City in the Clouds *somewhere behind the ranges!*

4. Lost City in the Clouds

More than a year had passed. It was the summer of 1910. One day Bingham ran into a wealthy college classmate, Edward S. Harkness, a collector of Peruvian documents. Harkness had heard of Bingham's enthusiasm for the Andes and offered to pay the expenses of a geologist to go along with Bingham when he next went to Peru.

Bingham was tremendously excited, and that winter, at a meeting of the Yale Club in New York City, he was describing his hopes and plans to a group of friends. On the spot, several of them, interested in various scientific fields, offered to sponsor a mountain-climbing expert, a naturalist, and a surgeon for a full-fledged expedition.

As the organizer and first fund-raiser for the trip, Bingham was named its director, and the Yale Peruvian Expedition of 1911 began to take shape. The members agreed that the purpose of the expedition would be to collect geological and biological data and possibly to scale several of the highest peaks in the Americas, peaks located south of the Cradle of Gold and estimated to reach 23,000 feet.

But Hiram Bingham would not be staying with the mountain-climbers. His goal was the elusive Inca city in the clouds.

He set out to read everything he could find about Peru and the Incas. He carefully reread the classic *History of the Conquest of Peru* by the nineteenth-century Boston historian William H. Prescott, and realized with a shock how few clues he would have to guide him in his search. Prescott had based his book on an account by Garcilasso de la Vega, son of a Spanish father and an Inca mother, an account written in the seventeenth century in Spain to present the people of Peru in the best possible light to a European audience. Garcilasso had left Peru for Spain in his teens, never to return, and wrote his chronicle as an old man—it was colorful but no doubt full of misinformation.

The Spaniards first began recording Inca history in 1532. There were many chronicles, written in the 1500s and 1600s by Spanish missionaries, soldiers, and government officials, but these were vague and often contradictory. The Spaniards tended to look down on the native people of the Andes and viewed them with either contempt or pity.

The Incas themselves had no written history, no account of their life and times from their own point of view. Bingham realized he would have to find clues on his own, like so many bits and pieces of broken pottery! He concluded that the Peruvians who believed the Cradle of Gold was the last Inca refuge were wrong. After all, how could it be the "lost city" when everybody had always known where it was, even if few people ever got there?

June 1911. Bingham and his fellow scholars sailed from New York for Lima, the capital of Peru. On arrival in Lima, Bingham went to confer with Don Carlos A. Romero, the official historian of the Spanish-colonial city.

The two historians studied maps made by Antonio Raimondi, a Peruvian geographer and explorer who had traveled all over Peru some fifty years earlier. Raimondi's maps showed many Inca ruins, but none at all in the valley of the Urubamba River, beyond the ruined Inca fortress of Ollantaytambo. Yet the Urubamba valley was only fifty or sixty miles from Cuzco—how strange that the Incas had not settled there. Or had they?

Romero showed Bingham two recently discovered documents, one written by a Spanish soldier who had gone gold-prospecting after the death of the last Inca emperor in 1572, another a biography of the first exiled emperor, Manco II, written by one of his sons. Bingham also took notes from a seventeenth-century Spanish chronicle by a monk named Antonio de Calancha, based on first-hand reports by monks who had actually managed to live and work near one remote mountain sanctuary of the last Incas. From these writings there appeared some evidence that the secret city would be found beyond the mountain ranges, in a region as yet unexplored and uncharted!

"I agree with you, Professor Bingham," Romero declared. "Choq-quequirau does not fit the descriptions of the location of the last Inca refuge. I suspect it was but one of a number of outposts of the Inca state in the forty years between Pizarro's invasion and its final downfall."

"How can I get to the Urubamba valley?" asked Bingham. "I was under the impression that it was completely inaccessible."

"And so it has been for nearly 400 years. Charles Wiener, a French explorer, tried to follow up rumors of Inca ruins at places then recorded as Huaina-Picchu and Matcho-Picchu in 1875, but was unable to pass the rapids and cliffs beyond the canyon. Actually, there was a way there, but it was over an extremely dangerous Inca road that ascends to a stormy pass at 15,200 feet between four-mile-high peaks—a pass closed by blizzards for all but a few weeks of the year. The canyon itself has always been blocked by 2,000-foot cliffs."

"I see—so we can't say *completely* inaccessible, because there is the *Inca road!*" Bingham exclaimed.

"Exactly—and better than that. You see, fifteen years ago there was a revival of the old rubber plantations in the Amazon jungle beyond the mountains, and for easier access to this region the government of Peru had a trail blasted along the sheer granite cliff face that had closed the Urubamba valley below Ollantaytambo," Romero explained. "So now you will be able to see for yourself whether our hunch is correct: that the Incas once lived in that remote valley."

"This Urubamba country—it must be very beautiful."

"Incredible, Professor Bingham—lush, tropical. Why, the word 'Urubamba' means 'flat-land-where-there-are-caterpillars,' " laughed Romero.

"Hmm," said Bingham. "Would it be too farfetched to guess that the valley may have been given its name by a people to whom caterpillars were something unusual? By a people from the cold highlands?"

"It is possible, Professor Bingham. But let me remind you that even if, as you suggest, a highland people from a cool climate might have reached the tropical Urubamba, we must not assume they would choose to settle there."

Bingham knew that this was true. Nevertheless, he could hardly wait to leave for Urubamba, to find out for himself.

*   *   *

44

The Yale Expedition members soon prepared to go their various ways. The mountain climbers left on their trek, and Bingham went to Cuzco to start his journey of discovery. With him were a naturalist, Harry Ward Foote, who planned to collect insect specimens, and a surgeon, Dr. William G. Erving. They left Cuzco by mule train in mid-July.

Crossing a cold plateau, they had an enchanting view of a valley paradise planted with grain, strawberries, roses, and lilies, and orchards of apples, peaches, and pears. Their guides told them it was Yucay, summer home of the last Inca emperors, visited by Spaniards in the years after the Conquest. The party spent a couple of days at Ollantaytambo, a modern Spanish town built on the ruins of the ancient Inca fortress. It was a sleepy place, shaded by poplars and willows, at the foot of magnificent mountains.

Here was the heart of Inca land, the place where they reached the dirt trail that would lead them into the Urubamba valley, a wilderness where virtually no one had set foot for the past 400 years! Only in the past few years had a few Indian farmers begun to settle there.

Precipices, churning rapids, low terraces of yucca and bananas, higher terraces with maize, potatoes, and coca, fields of orchids, tree ferns, bamboo—it was a land of savage contrasts, for towering above were the ever-present glassy blue glaciers with the clouds hovering over their summits.

Barely fifty miles from Cuzco! It was a wonderland, a dream world, this canyon of the Urubamba.

On July 23, Bingham, Foote, Erving, and their guides pitched camp on a little plain by the river. Their presence aroused the curiosity of a tenant farmer and mule driver who owned a grass-thatched hut nearby. Bingham introduced himself and explained that he was looking for Inca ruins.

"Oh yes, Señor, there are some fine buildings on top of the mountain across the river." The farmer pointed straight up. "There is a great city on the ridge of Huayna Picchu."

A great city? Huayna Picchu! The place the French explorer had tried in vain to reach! Bingham stared up at the green sugarloaf peak and turned to the farmer.

"Will you take me there in the morning?"

The farmer shrugged. "Perhaps," he said.

That night Bingham slept fitfully, and rushed to the farmer's hut very early, in a cold, drizzling rain.

"It is much too hard a climb for such a wet day," the farmer announced flatly. Bingham offered him a *sol* (about fifty cents, but three or four times the farmer's usual daily wage) and the farmer changed his mind.

Bingham asked Foote and Erving if they wanted to come along.

"Not me, Hiram," said Foote. "I've seen too many unusual butterflies right here in the canyon, and when it stops raining I want to be around to gather specimens."

"Count me out, too," said the surgeon. "This trek has been hard on the gear. I'll just catch up on the mending and maybe do some laundry. But good luck anyway!"

So Bingham shook hands with his colleagues all around and turned to the farmer and a Quechua-speaking army sergeant who had been escorting them. "Let's go!"

The three began a 45-minute climb along the main road upstream, through a haunt of poisonous snakes, between the cliff faces, and then, beyond the canyon, undertook the descent through a sodden jungle to the icy rapids. The two Andeans nimbly crossed the plunging current over a primitive bridge of four logs lashed together with vines. Bingham crawled across six inches at a time on his hands and knees.

Then they struggled on all fours for more than an hour and a half up through the jungle growth on the opposite bank, in a steaming rain forest in the wettest part of Peru. They were just five hard days' trek from Cuzco, a distance of only sixty miles, yet the heat and humidity at the lower altitude were almost unbearable.

And there were no ruins in sight.

Around noon, completely exhausted, they came to a cluster of huts some 2,000 feet above the river. The Indians who inhabited the tiny settlement were surprised but pleased to have visitors, and offered the strangers cold boiled potatoes for lunch, along with gourds filled with cool water. Two men introduced themselves as Richarte and Alvarez, farmers who had moved to the isolated spot four years earlier.

"The new government road has made it easier for people to settle here," the farmers said, "although in the rainy season we can leave the valley only by the old road over the precipices."

As Bingham surveyed the terraces of maize, potatoes, sugar cane, beans, peppers, and tomatoes, he considered that it was more than likely the canyon had once been inhabited, though not for the past several hundred years. As a secret hideaway for exiled emperors, it would have offered a semi-tropical setting for farming, rich soil, and nights cold enough to freeze-dry the *papas*, or white potatoes, used to make *chuñu*, the staple food of the Andes.

After lunch, while the farmers and their wives and the sergeant gossiped by the huts, Bingham took a few minutes to relax on a wooden bench the Indians had draped with a soft woollen poncho. It was cool, and the view was splendid. The sugarloaf peaks were handsome, but he was dead tired and disappointed, afraid that the so-called "great city" would be little more than a few ruined stone houses. Still, this was no time to give up. He pulled himself to his feet and rounded a promontory.

Before him there rose a breathtakingly beautiful flight of contoured terraces on the hillside, perhaps one hundred of them, and each one hundreds of feet long and about ten feet high. They had recently been partially cleared. Terraces like these were common both at the Cradle of Gold and at Ollantaytambo—known to be very important Inca settlements!

The Indian farmers had hacked out a little path up the hill, and anchored it with vine and tree-trunk ladders. Bingham quickly scaled it and moments later, amid a jungle-covered maze of walls, he found himself examining white granite blocks of the finest, most precise Inca construction, cut and fitted without a trace of mortar.

Roughly cleared by the farmers, the place spread out under a thicket of bamboo, vines, moss, and small gnarled trees. It was not a ruin, but an almost perfectly preserved city!

The nameless city, virtually unconquerable on its perch between two peaks, contained hardly any open space. Every inch seemed to have been put to use. On an overhanging ledge, the outer wall of a semicircular building gracefully followed the curve of the natural rock foundation. Where had he seen a wall like that before? Suddenly he remembered: the magnificent foundation wall of the Church of Santo Domingo in Cuzco, known to be the wall of the sacred Temple of the Sun!

Another fine wall of white granite, unadorned on the outside, had large wall pegs and niches on the inside—it was clearly an important

structure, perhaps another temple. These niches once held the mummies of royal ancestors, and on the pegs had hung great jars of ceremonial *chicha*.

Spellbound, Bingham climbed a flight of steps up a steep incline. Next to a little vegetable garden the two Indian farmers had planted, he saw a majestic stairway of huge stone blocks, small plazas, ledges wide and narrow, alleyways every which-way, and stone-lined watercourses. And wherever he looked, steps and more steps!

Two stunning rectangular palaces or temples faced a central courtyard, each with three walls and thus open on the side facing the court. The foundation stones were taller than a man. Across the court stood a strange wall with three windows that faced the ridge over which the sun

rose. Bingham recalled one of the Spanish chronicles, written in the 1600s, in which there were tales of a unique and mysterious wall with three windows at a place in Peru where earthquakes were said to be unknown.

Joyfully, Bingham realized that he had stumbled, with incredible luck, on a fantastic discovery. Chronicles, maps, clues, legends—all faded before this wonderful reality. Ghost-like wisps of cloud hovered over the taller mountain peak of Huayna Picchu. Its lower twin, Machu Picchu, stood like a sentry above the narrow ravine where, 2,000 feet below, the green Urubamba thundered around a hairpin bend to surround the dream city on three sides.

Invisible from the valley below, it was a city without a name, and Bingham decided to call it Machu Picchu. Miracle of miracles in this rainy season, today the sun was shining, and as he raised his camera to

51

take the photographs that would later prove, even to himself, that this city of secrets was real, Bingham thought of the divine voice that spurred on Kipling's "Explorer":

Anybody might have found it, but—His Whisper
came to Me!

5. Sanctuary of the Sun

Bingham was unable to clear and explore his dream city alone, so he pressed on, during the few weeks that followed, deep into the uncharted range of mountains. He was searching for Inca sites that could help confirm that Machu Picchu was the lost city known as Vilcapampa the Old, the secret capital of the last Inca state.

On August 8, he tentatively identified one ruined hilltop in the valley of the Vilcabamba River as Vitcos, the last military headquarters of the Incas, a place known as the Hill of Roses and twice destroyed by the Spaniards in battle. He knew this identification was correct when, the next day, he rediscovered a legendary white rock shrine nearby, a shrine often mentioned in chronicles as Yurak Rumi, the most sacred place in the shrunken remnant of the empire after the Spanish Conquest.

After his return to the United States with the other members of the Yale Peruvian Expedition, Bingham could think of little else but Machu Picchu, for the one day he had spent there had changed his life. Dazzled by its beauty and convinced of its importance, he began to make plans to explore the city.

He returned to Peru in the summer of 1912, with an expedition sponsored by Yale University and the National Geographic Society, to clear the city of jungle growth, map it carefully, and undertake thorough excavations. For the very first time, an Inca city was to be explored and described by scholars and archaeologists—not dismantled by treasure hunters or by Spaniards and Indians seeking building materials.

With great hardship, Bingham's engineers and their Indian laborers built a new trail for bearers to carry up food and supplies and carry out pottery and other finds. They would have to travel on foot, for no llama or mule could possibly use the near-vertical path that zig-zagged (with steps here and there) up the snake-infested hillside to the city.

The city itself was entangled in the toughest brushwood and mesquite. Hardwood trees two feet thick grew on top of the gable ends of some houses. It took several months for the work crew to cut away the overgrowth, burn the debris, and painstakingly clean the moss from the polished walls and carved rocks. Once cut away, the jungle vegetation immediately began to spread again, so fast that scrub and bamboo had to be cut back three more times in four months.

The Urubamba River's booming voice echoed to the top of the canyon walls, just one part of the city's remarkable natural defenses. The razor-like ridge that led into the city was only forty feet across, and Bingham guessed that two men with slings and stones could have held the path against an army. The sheer drops of 1,500 feet to the east and west of the ridge would have permitted the Inca soldiers to roll boulders down on would-be attackers. Signal towers on the two peaks commanded views for miles. As Bingham lay flat on his stomach to take photographs from the dizzy ramparts, two Indians held fast to his legs—for the next solid ground was 2,500 feet down.

A dry moat faced with stones ran across the ridge next to the south cliff and marked the narrowest part of the ridge. An outer wall edged magnificent terraces, and an inner wall guarded the city proper on the only side accessible by an ancient road. The city gate, now an open doorway, appeared to have once been closed by a heavy door barred with a cross-log, for there were great stone rings on either side. No one entered the city against the emperor's will—it would simply not have been possible.

The main thoroughfare of the city began at this gate at the south end, divided the city in two parts, and continued to the cliff face that rose up to the northeast. Space was severely limited on the ridge, and houses had been cleverly crowded together. Every inch of space had been set aside for some use—tucked behind each house was a tiny garden plot only a few feet square.

All the districts of the city were linked by a fascinating web of stairs, side streets, and tiny alleys. Bingham counted more than one hundred rockhewn stairways of all sizes, from three or four steps to 150 or more. A great flight of steps in the heart of the city bordered the main watercourse, so Bingham called it the Stairway of the Fountains. A narrow watercourse not four inches wide carried water from springs on Machu Picchu mountain along a terrace and through four stone basins south of the great stairway, which then divided around a catch-basin. The water then ran on through twelve more shallow "fountains."

The city was divided into groups of dwellings of six to ten houses each, probably for extended families or clans. Each compound had a common entrance, which could be barred. Most houses were of the typical steeply gabled type with ringstones to hold rafters and thatches. Bingham called this district the East City.

The south end had the most beautiful dwellings. There Bingham found some ruined houses of stone and clay and two rough stone terraces, and wondered if Manco II might have erected them in haste after his escape from Cuzco. The rest of the city seemed very much older and finer.

Overlooking the highest of the sixteen fountains was the Temple of the Sun, the semicircular building Bingham had so admired on the day he discovered the citadel. Adjoining this temple was a supremely graceful and finely cut wall which he called the Beautiful Wall. Scrubbed clean, it proved to be smoother and more lustrous than any he had ever seen.

Under the Beautiful Wall was a cave with finely cut niches. The wall itself, resting on a natural rock base, had held together for hundreds, perhaps thousands of years. Its interior face was as smoothly polished as its exterior. In this wall there was an unusually placed window, one Bingham could not compare to any other. The building did remind him of the temple at Cuzco, and he wondered if the window, from which there was a panoramic view, had been the place where the priests had hung the huge golden image of the Sun God, facing east to catch their protector's first rays at daybreak. It was a genuine puzzle—he called it the Problematical Window.

Below the temple wall, Bingham's crew dug up more than 200 nicely

decorated pots, all broken. Bingham thought the spot might have been a rubbish dump for vessels used in religious ceremonies.

The building Bingham called the Principal Temple faced the Sacred Plaza. It had three walls, and was open facing the plaza. Bingham believed that it had never had a roof, but possibly had been covered at times with a woven canopy over a wooden beam, to let in sunlight but screen the temple rituals from view. In back, there seemed to be a large altar of stone. Bingham knew that the Incas used no preservatives or spices in mummifying their royal dead, and he speculated that here in the damp climate of the eastern slopes of the Andes, the mummies would have needed frequent drying-out in the sun. In this temple, perhaps, they were displayed in rows.

To the east stood the exciting Temple of the Three Windows, also walled on three sides only and open to the sky. The windows were in the back wall, revealing a spectacular view.

Not far from the great stairway, the crew uncovered buildings with solid walls almost as fine as the Beautiful Wall. Since this was the only compound grand enough to serve as a royal residence, Bingham called it the King's Group. The entrance to the compound was close to the highest of the sixteen fountains. Oddly, the upper stories, in contrast to the lower walls, were roughly plastered and thatched, and the gables were unusually steep. Could these buildings have been altered to prevent semitropical downpours from soaking through thatched roofs? Perhaps by a band of refugees from Cuzco? Many of the buildings at Machu Picchu—some 200 of them—had windows, yet the King's Group did not!

Bingham began to feel that while parts of the city were Inca, even late Inca, other areas were much more ancient.

From the Sacred Plaza a grand flight of steps, each cut from a single block of stone and about four feet wide, led to the Sacred Hill, in the northwest corner of the city. There Bingham found a small gem of a temple, and by this temple an *Intihuatana,* a Hitching Post of the Sun. The top of the boulder had obviously been cut away and squared off, and it showed *no sign of damage!* This tall sundial had survived just as the

Incas had made it—proof to Bingham that no Spaniard had ever set foot in Machu Picchu!

Bingham was thrilled as he had never been before! This stunning city, invisible from the valley just below, had stood silent and unsuspected since the unknown day on which its last inhabitant had gone to a mysterious fate.

With renewed energy and excitement, Bingham and his colleagues began digging in various areas to discover whatever they could about these last inhabitants. By the city gate, Bingham found piles of sling stones. So it had been a military garrison! In the south and east parts of the city, he found jugs and food dishes, in about equal quantities, indicating that those districts had been residential. Not far from the city gate, however, Bingham's crew found fragments of forty-one large jars and nine drinking dippers, but only four cooking pots and not one food dish. Here the *chicha* beer vendors must have had their stands!

Virtually all the pottery fragments and utensils found were classic Inca. Many hammerstones were found too. The Indian helpers Bingham had brought from Cuzco were eager to discover treasure, and they cheerfully thumped temple floors with their crowbars to detect hollow-sounding places. They found no bronze tools, no pots, and not one bone in any of the temples, nor any of the legendary gold objects. They carefully replaced the dirt over their fruitless "digs."

After a week of disappointment, Bingham consulted local Indians familiar with the area. He offered a *sol* to the man who could show him a burial cave. The Indians, not uninterested in treasure themselves, promptly led Bingham not to one but eight, all down the wooded slope on the east side of the ridge, facing the rising sun.

Bingham worked together with Dr. George F. Eaton, the expedition's osteologist, or expert on bones. Dr. Eaton photographed each grave entrance, then opened it, carefully measured it, and diagramed the position of the skeleton and any other objects such as pottery, tools, ornaments, or animal bones. Such objects would offer clues to the Incas' belief in an afterlife and also to the identity of the dead person.

The first grave yielded the bones of a woman, buried in the customary Andean sitting position, along with some pots and dishes. The second, perhaps once raided by animals, held only bone fragments. A third, also of a woman, contained Bingham's first perfect piece of Inca pottery, a nicely decorated two-handled dish.

The crew went over the whole ridge, and opened about one hundred graves, all more or less overgrown, on very steep slopes. Bingham believed that the graves were on the slopes because land for cultivation was too scarce within Inca cities to be spared for cemeteries. All the graves seemed to have been dug under ledges, or in caves, where they were somewhat protected from rain. The best remains were found in those few caves that had been roughly walled in.

Over the years, in the damp climate, cloth had rotted and mummy bundles had tumbled open. Many graves contained fire-blackened cooking pots, possessions women would need in the afterlife. Scattered in most caves were llama bones, usually split so that the marrow would provide food for the dead. Bingham speculated that they were the bones of llamas grown too old and frail to carry loads, for the Incas valued their llama herds too much to consume them as food.

One grave was clearly that of a noblewoman, possibly, Bingham thought, a high priestess. Buried with her remains were two jugs and a stewpot, bits of woollen cloth, two large shawl pins, two thorn sewing needles, tweezers, a tiny spoon, a bronze mirror, and the skeleton of a little dog.

Nearly all the graves in the cemetery were of females. In another cemetery, near the end of the outer city wall, the same thing was true. In fact, of the remains of 175 people, about 150 were identified as female!

Hiram Bingham concluded that Machu Picchu had been, in its last years, a kind of convent dedicated to the Sun God. Since it would have required the services of farmers, woodchoppers, water-carriers, and soldier-defenders, Bingham theorized that such persons, presumably men, had been buried in less holy ground, farther from the sanctuary itself.

The fate of the inhabitants of Machu Picchu remains a mystery. Did they abandon the city abruptly? Or did they live out their lives in peace, solitude, and safety, dying one by one until there was no one left within those eerie walls? We shall probably never know.

Today orchids and wild flowers grace the ancient terraces, like bright jewels. Tiny lizards dart over the smooth stones and sun themselves in the niches of deserted temples and palaces. Where priests once worshiped the Sun God at the moment of daybreak, llamas graze peacefully, their green pastures nourished by the mists that rise from the river and by the golden rays of the faithful sun.

Epilogue

By the time he wrote his last book about the Lost City in the Clouds, in 1948, Hiram Bingham had concluded that after the Spaniards conquered Peru, the last of the ruling Incas maintained an independent state in the remote fastnesses of the Urubamba valley for thirty-five years. They had two capitals, Bingham surmised—a military stronghold (known to the Spaniards) at Vitcos, and a hidden sanctuary at Vilcapampa.

Bingham was certain that the spectacular city he had discovered high on a ridge below the peak of Machu Picchu was this sacred retreat of Vilcapampa. He believed that it had been lost for centuries precisely because it was located in the most inaccessible corner of the most inaccessible mountain chain of the Central Andes—though it was a mere sixty miles from Cuzco!

After Bingham and his team had excavated and cleared the site in 1912, the jungle once more took over the citadel of Machu Picchu, and it was not until 1934 that the Peruvian government once again decided to clear their "national treasure." Like so many exciting ruins, notably the Mayan ruins in the Yucatán of Mexico, it had quickly become thickly overgrown, for, as Bingham once observed, Machu Picchu's only real enemy was the jungle.

In his explorations and excavations between 1912 and 1915, Hiram Bingham demonstrated that the Urubamba valley had once been thickly populated. The area had clearly been well connected by a number of roads to other important Inca settlements and to Cuzco.

This was confirmed in 1940-1941 by the North American Wenner-Gren Scientific Expedition, which cleared, mapped, and rephotographed the sites in the Urubamba region that had been explored by Bingham more than twenty-five years earlier.

Bingham was convinced that the civilization of the Andes was very old. He reasoned that it would have taken thousands of years for the people of highland Peru to have domesticated their astonishingly wide variety of food and medicinal plants, each specially adapted to cultivation at greatly differing altitudes. Similarly, it would have taken them many centuries to domesticate the llama as a beast of burden and the alpaca as a source of wool—both from the same wild ancestor, the camel-like guanaco.

Bingham speculated that originally Machu Picchu had even been the capital of an ancient pre-Inca kingdom whose surviving population had kept alive the wisdom of their ancestors during a "dark age" of barbarian invasions by tribes from the Amazon jungle.

Hiram Bingham was a pioneer, a tireless adventurer, and a man with a vivid imagination and a sense of history—yet he was not a professional scientist. Despite his energy and his careful scholarship, his conclusions and theories were often questioned by others.

In 1964-1965, North American members of the Andean Explorers' Club visited a place deep in the rain forests of the Amazon headwaters where Bingham had stopped briefly in August 1911, after his discovery of Machu Picchu. At this place, Espiritu Pampa, Plain of the Ghosts, where Bingham had assumed there was nothing but jungle, the modern explorers found the sprawling ruins of a huge city: some 300 dwellings, a grand temple, fifty or sixty carefully constructed large buildings, a "long palace," and traces of Inca roads. There were broken pots and jars and, most intriguing, piles of curved red roof tiles apparently made by native Peruvians in crude imitation of the Spanish-style tiles the European conquerors were using in Cuzco. (Bingham had, in fact, noticed a few of these tiles in 1911.) There were many buildings made of fieldstone set in clay, which suggested that the great city of Espiritu Pampa might have been a makeshift hideout, built in a hurry. Situated at only 3,000 feet in altitude, unusually low for an Inca city, it could have been the royal residence that a son of Manco II, the exiled emperor, had once described as being "in a warm climate." (The same prince had referred also to a royal city "in a cold district," probably the military-political capital, Vitcos.)

Some scholars believe that Espiritu Pampa is more likely than Machu Picchu to be the city known as Vilcapampa the Old. It was probably near this jungle city that the youngest son of Manco II was finally tracked down by Spanish soldiers in 1572. The Spanish marched him back to Cuzco in chains and executed him, and so the great Inca civilization was no more.

Other scholars are now reconsidering Hiram Bingham's theories and trying to determine whether Machu Picchu was indeed merely one of many Inca outposts, or something far more significant. The mystery may never be solved—but while the Inca civilization seemed to vanish into thin air more than 400 years ago, the sacred Lost City in the Clouds is a silent witness to its memory.

GLOSSARY

ALPACA   Small domesticated camel of South America, related to the llama. It is raised for its wool, and has never been successfully raised elsewhere.

ALTIPLANO   High, bleak plateau in Bolivia, near Lake Titicaca.

ANDES   Highest mountain range in the Western hemisphere, running the full length of western South America, from the isthmus of Panama to Cape Horn.

BOLÍVAR, SIMÓN   A South American revolutionary hero (1783-1830).

BORLA   The sacred crown-like red fringe worn by Inca emperors.

CHICHA   A beer made from crushed and boiled sprouted maize (Indian corn), drunk by everyone in the Andes.

CHUÑU   White potatoes, which are native to the Andes, preserved by freeze-drying; a staple food both in Inca times and today.

COCA   A tropical bush whose narcotic leaves can be chewed as a painkiller or for the relief of fatigue.

CONDOR   A very large vulture of the high Andes.

CONQUISTADOR   A leader in the Spanish conquest of America, especially of Mexico and Peru during the 16th Century.

CORDILLERA   Mountain range.

CUY   A native rodent of the Andes, domesticated to varying sizes and colors; known elsewhere as the "guinea pig," though it is neither from Guinea nor a pig.

CUZCO   Ancient Inca capital in the Andes at an altitude of 11,200 feet above sea level; now a modern town of about 60,000 inhabitants.

INCA   King, lord, emperor; also refers, today, to a civilization.

INTIHUATANA   Sundial, "place to which the sun is tied," or "hitching post of the sun."

INTI-RAYMI   "Sun-dance," the festival of Midwinter's Day, celebrated in late June (because the seasons are reversed in the Southern Hemisphere).

LLAMA   Small, frail, domesticated camel of South America, related to the alpaca. It is raised as a pack animal, and has never been raised successfully elsewhere. If it is overloaded, it will kneel and refuse to move; it can carry, at most, eighty to a hundred pounds.

PAPAS   White potatoes, tubers native to the Andes.

QUECHUA   Official language of the Inca empire, still spoken by ten million people (pronounced "ketch-wa").

QUIPU   "Knot string," a tally or ledger used by the Incas in a complex decimal counting system decipherable only by trained "readers"; the only system of "writing" the Incas used.

SOL   "Sun," a Peruvian silver dollar worth about fifty cents in Bingham's time.

TITICACA   The world's highest navigable lake, at 12,500 feet, shared by Peru and Bolivia; also, the legendary birthplace of the first Inca rulers.

IMPORTANT DATES

1200 ? A.D.   Manco Capac founds the Inca dynasty in Cuzco.

1438–1471   Reign of Emperor Pachacuti.

1471–1493   Reign of Topa Inca.

1476 ?   Francisco Pizarro is born in Trujillo, Spain.

1492   Christopher Columbus discovers America.

1493–1527   Reign of Huayna Capac.

1524–1525   Pizarro sails along the coast of Peru.

1527   Pizarro makes a second voyage to Peru.

1529   King Philip II of Spain awards Pizarro the right of discovery and
                conquest for Peru.

1532   Pizarro lands on the coast of Peru and captures Atahualpa, son of
                Huayna Capac.

1534   Cuzco falls to Pizarro.

1534–1545 ?   Reign of Manco II.

1535   Pizarro founds a new capital at Lima.

1536	Manco II stages an unsuccessful rebellion, then escapes to found a kingdom-in-exile in a secret location.
1541	Pizarro is assassinated in Lima.
1545–1560	Reign of Sayri Tupac, eldest son of Manco II.
1560–1571	Reign of Titu Cusi, Manco's second son. Titu Cusi dictates an account of the Spanish Conquest and the life and death of his father, Manco II, to a Spanish monk.
1571–1572	Reign of Tupac Amaru, Manco's third son and the last Inca emperor. Tupac Amaru is captured and put to death by the Spaniards.
1860s	Antonio Raimondi, Peruvian geographer, explores most of Peru and maps remote Inca provinces.
1875	Hiram Bingham is born on November 19 in the Hawaiian Islands.
1895	The Peruvian government builds a road through the canyon of the Urubamba.
1898	Hiram Bingham graduates from Yale College.
1906	Bingham visits South America for the first time.
1908–1909	Bingham is an official delegate to the first Pan American Scientific Congress in Santiago, Chile, and then visits Choqquequirau.
1911	Yale Peruvian Expedition and Bingham's discovery of a nameless Inca city that he calls Machu Picchu.
1912	Bingham leads an expedition co-sponsored by Yale and the National Geographic Society to clear and excavate at Machu Picchu.

1915	Bingham leads an expedition to explore in the vicinity of Machu Picchu and finds ancient roads linking it to Ollantaytambo, Vitcos, and Cuzco.
1925–1933	Bingham, after being elected governor of Connecticut (and serving for a day only) fills the seat of a U.S. Senator and then is elected to a full term in Congress.
1928	Railroad tracks are laid from Cuzco to Machu Picchu, a distance of 66 miles.
1934	Machu Picchu is cleared again by the Peruvian government to commemorate it as a "national treasure" on the 400th anniversary of the Spanish Conquest.
1941–1942	The Wenner-Gren Expedition clears, maps, and photographs Machu Picchu and finds new Inca towns in the region.
1948	An automobile road to Machu Picchu is constructed.
1956	Hiram Bingham dies on June 6, at the age of 80, in Washington, D.C.

MUSEUMS

Many museums of art and natural history have South American departments. Ask for the Pre-Columbian collections—the arts of the Americas before Columbus—and look for pottery, textiles, jewelry, sculpture, weapons, tools, ceremonial objects, architectural models, and many other interesting articles. The following museums have Peruvian collections in particular.

American Museum of Natural History, New York, N.Y.

Art Institute of Chicago, Illinois (pottery)

Brooklyn Museum, Brooklyn, N.Y.

Davenport Public Museum, Iowa

Denver Art Museum, Colorado

Dumbarton Oaks Research Library and Collections, Washington, D.C.

Metropolitan Museum of Art, New York, N.Y. (feather-work)

Museum of the American Indian, New York, N.Y.

Ohio Wesleyan University, Columbus, Art Hall (pottery)

Textile Museum, Washington, D.C.

University of California at Davis Art Gallery

University of Illinois, Champaign-Urbana, Krannert Art Museum

SELECTED BIBLIOGRAPHY

Baumann, Hans. *Gold and Gods of Peru*. New York, Pantheon, 1963.
  Vivid recreation of Inca culture.

Beck, Barbara L. *The First Book of the Incas*. New York, Franklin Watts, 1966.
  Several of the illustrations, by Page Cary, have been redrawn from a sixteenth-century Inca-Spanish chronicle.

Bierhorst, John. *Black Rainbow: Legends of the Incas and Myths of Ancient Peru*. Farrar, Straus & Giroux, 1976.
  Twenty selections, illustrated by Jane Byers Bierhorst.

Bingham, Hiram. "In the Wonderland of Peru," *National Geographic*, April 1913, pp. 387-573.
  Bingham's report of his first excavations at Machu Picchu, with fine black-and-white photographs on almost every page.

*——— *Lost City of the Incas*. New York, Duell, Sloan and Pearce, 1948; Atheneum paperback, 1963.
  Bingham's summation of several earlier books about his explorations in Peru. Illustrated with about sixty photographs, most by Bingham himself.

Bleeker, Sonia. *The Inca: Indians of the Andes*. New York, William Morrow, 1960.
  By the author of numerous books about Indians of the Americas.

Burland, C. A. *Peru Under the Incas*. New York, Putnam's, 1968.
  In the "Life in Ancient Lands" series.

Eiseman, Alberta. *Candido*. New York, Macmillan, 1965.
  A picture book, with illustrations by Lilian Obligado, about Paco, a boy of the Andes, and his pet llama, Candido, who must learn to do his share of the work in a llama caravan that carries potatoes to market.

Glubok, Shirley. *Art of Ancient Peru*. New York, Harper & Row, 1966.
  A volume in a highly praised art series for young readers.

*Hemming, John. *The Conquest of the Incas*. New York, Harcourt Brace Jovanovich, 1970.
  A long and scholarly account, with excellent maps and many fascinating photographs.

Howard, Cecil, and the editors of *Horizon* magazine. *Pizarro and the Conquest of Peru*. New York, Harper-Crest/American Heritage, 1968.
  Richly illustrated in color.

*Johnson, William Weber, and the editors of Time-Life Books. *The Andean Republics: Bolivia, Chile, Ecuador, Peru*. New York, Time-Life Books, 1965.
  In the "Life World Library" series, dealing mainly with geography and contemporary history. Exciting photographs of Machu Picchu and Andean scenery and daily life.

McIntyre, Loren. *The Incredible Incas and Their Timeless Land*. Washington, National Geographic Society, 1975.
  Lavishly illustrated.

———. "Lost Empire of the Incas," *National Geographic*, December 1973, pp. 729-787.
  Stunning color photographs include aerial views of Machu Picchu and the surrounding countryside. Also, an artist's rendering of Cuzco at the height of the Inca empire, and a tapestry-like picture panorama of the fall of the Incas to Pizarro.

Masters, Robert V. *Peru in Pictures*. New York, Sterling, 1973.
In the "Visual Geography" series. Full-color cover photograph of Machu Picchu and several interesting black-and-white views of Inca roads and agricultural terraces.

*Prescott, William H. *History of the Conquest of Peru*. New York, Modern Library, 1936; NAL-Mentor paperback, 1961, abridged by Victor W. Von Hagen.
Classic history of the Spanish Conquest, first published in 1847.

*Rodman, Selden. *Peru Traveler*. New York, Meredith, 1967.
A modern travel book that includes photographs of Hiram Bingham in 1912 and a fine photograph of the intact sundial at Machu Picchu.

*Von Hagen, Victor W. *Highway of the Sun*. Duell, Sloan and Pearce, 1955.
Good modern photographs, by a well-known explorer, of Inca roads and buildings.

*———, ed. *The Incas of Pedro Cieza de León*. Norman, University of Oklahoma Press, 1959.
Scholarly translation and edition of a sixteenth-century chronicle that includes fine photographs of Inca sites, woodcuts from old Spanish books, and a reproduction of the engraving of the bridge over the Apurímac River (the Great Speaker) that helped persuade Hiram Bingham to visit Peru (between pp. 144–145).

Wilder, Thornton. *The Bridge of San Luis Rey*. New York, Harper & Row, 1967; Washington Square Press/Simon & Schuster paperback.
A short, suspenseful novel, first published in 1927, about five strangers who lost their lives, by strange coincidence, in the collapse of the famous 500-year-old rope suspension bridge over the Apurímac River.

*Books best suited to adult readers.

ELIZABETH GEMMING is the author of more than a dozen books for young people, including *Born in a Barn, Maple Harvest,* and *Wool Gathering*—all for Coward, McCann & Geoghegan. A graduate of Wellesley College, Mrs. Gemming lives in New Haven, Connecticut, with her husband, Klaus, a book designer, and their two children, Marianne and Christina.

MIKE EAGLE, a graduate of Hartford Art School at the University of Hartford, is a freelance illustrator whose work has appeared in books, magazines, and advertising. Mr. Eagle lives in Old Saybrook, Connecticut, with his wife, Mary, and their children, Michael and Christian.